The Sayings of Anthony Trollope

The Sayings of

ANTHONY
TROLLOPE

edited by

RICHARD MULLEN

DUCKWORTH

First published in 1992 by
Gerald Duckworth & Co. Ltd.
The Old Piano Factory
48 Hoxton Square, London N1 6PB
Tel: 071 729 5986
Fax: 071 729 0015

A catalogue record for this book is available
from the British Library

ISBN 0 7156 2420 2

Photoset in North Wales by
Derek Doyle & Associates, Mold, Clwyd
Printed in Great Britain by
Redwood Press Limited, Melksham

Contents

To the memory
of
Jean and Peter Gray

Introduction

Anthony Trollope's life and opinions make his novels and other works a rich source of memorable quotations. From his birth in 1815 until he became a Post Office clerk in 1834, he was under the influence of two formidable parents, each of whom was fond of quoting well-worn advice, his father from classical authors and eighteenth-century essayists, his mother from Dante, Molière and Byron. In addition, both parents made appeal to traditional phrases such as the need for 'elbow grease': an allusion that would turn up time and time again in their youngest son's novels.

The Victorians increasingly saw the novel as an effective way to influence people, particularly young readers, who formed such a large part of the audience for fiction. Once the novel became respectable, it needed to do more than entertain: it had to instruct as well as to pass the hours. Trollope, who studied fiction as well as writing it, said: 'No man or woman with a conscience ... can go on from year to year spinning stories without the desire of teaching.' If a writer wished to be responsible and respectable, he had to point to a lesson as quickly and as lightly as possible. This was what Trollope saw as sugar-coated medicine: 'Gentle readers, the physic is always beneath the sugar, hidden or unhidden. In writing novels we novelists preach to you from our pulpits.'

No other Victorian novelist pops up so often in his books to speak directly to 'gentle readers'. For some critics, notably Henry James, this is a severe fault. These authorial intrusions provide most of the sayings in this collection, and nothing is more characteristic of Trollope than his frequent pauses in narration to insert some short reflection or piece of pungent advice. These usually read like a hint from a wise uncle, who has seen much of life and is anxious to provide help mixed with humour for those still making their way along the path.

Most of Trollope's fiction features some young person reaching a turning point in life, usually the prospect of marriage. For Trollope – and his age – marriage was more important for the woman because it was virtually the only career to which most women could aspire. For his own part, he knew that his happiness and success dated from his happy marriage to Rose Heseltine in 1844. Thus many of his best sayings take the form of advice to the young about love and marriage. For young men there was an additional problem: they had to be bred up into gentlemen. This is a central theme of his fiction. Almost all of his forty-seven novels discuss what it means to be a gentleman, and the author often appears with a handy summation or with advice for readers.

Victorian gentlemen were supposed to be 'manly' and 'truthful', and there was no virtue that Trollope admired more than honesty. As a dedicated student of human nature he knew that most gentlemen occasionally lied. It is often thought that *The Way We Live Now* sprang from a sudden conviction on Trollope's part that England was being lured down dishonest paths. Yet he had been show-ing how dishonesty could ruin lives from his first novel, *The Macdermots of Ballycloran*, published in 1847. The central dilemma of the first Barsetshire novel, *The Warden*, features a clergyman confronting attacks on his honesty for taking too much money for too little work.

Trollope was a remarkably honest man and this is reflec-ted in his comments about himself. His *Autobiography* is one of the most truthful performances in that nebulous border-land between fact and fiction. His youthful misery and mature prosperity gave him a detailed knowledge of Vic-torian society and manners, which he reproduced with almost photographic precision in his fiction.

Many of Trollope's 'sayings' reflect what I have called elsewhere his 'divided mind', which saw that almost every question had at least two sides. His outlook on life was governed by a firm Christian faith. Traditional High Church Anglicanism provided not just the setting for his most memorable novels but the firm moral base on which his life rested. After the success of the six Barsetshire novels, he knew that readers expected reflections and quips about the clergy and the Church. These comments were usually meant to entertain, although some were designed to attack those he disliked or to promote a less rigid approach to theology. If his remarks on the Church and clergy were often light-hearted, his views on religion and human nature are central to Trollope the man. Indeed, one cannot really understand Trollope as a man or as a writer without seeing the importance of his religious views. He believed that most people were a curious amalgam of good and bad. Therefore everyone who desired to raise humanity must try to encourage the good. Novelists, who wrote the most influential 'sermons' of the age, had a particularly strong moral obligation not only to point readers in the right direction, but also to give some sympathy to those who had turned down the wrong path.

In spite of his vast output of fiction, Trollope wrote widely on politics and other serious topics. As an important official in the Post Office, responsible for the adoption of the pillar box, he took a strong interest in public affairs. His work in laying out postal routes gave him an insight into the lives of all sorts and conditions of people and a desire to improve the lot of ordinary folk. This was nowhere more the case than in Ireland, where he spent almost a third of his active life. When he stood for Parliament in 1867, he emphasised two issues: education for working-class children and justice for Ireland. Intellectually Trollope was a Liberal, but he had deep conservative instincts, best seen in his defence of hierarchical society and the Church of England.

Some facile critics have tended to dismiss Trollope as a boisterous 'word-smith' who churned out novels like clockwork and then spent the rest of the day fox hunting. Trollope did have a staggering ability to write by schedule. Most days, from 1847 until his death in 1882, saw him at his desk by dawn, and this discipline left a great amount of free time, some of which he certainly spent chasing foxes or playing whist at his clubs. However, he spent many more hours studying English literature and the great Latin authors. He was prouder of his *Life of Cicero* than of any of his other books.

He also learned a great deal from his travels, a passion which he inherited from his mother. Although Trollope travelled widely in Europe for pleasure, his visits to what he called 'the English world' had a more serious purpose. His travel books, *North America, Australia and New Zealand,* and *South Africa* were written to help Britons understand the new societies to which they had given birth as well as to act as guides for anyone wanting to settle there.

Trollope never set out to be a great stylist, let alone a writer of quips. Indeed his ever-present tendency towards wordiness makes some of his best comments too lengthy to be included in an anthology. Fortunately he was remarkably consistent in his ideas, and thus a shorter, more quotable version almost always turns up in another book. What emerges from this brief collection of some of his best sayings is a writer of great breadth and depth, a man who has reflected deeply on life and human nature and who hoped, in his writing, both to entertain his readers and to give them a gentle nudge in the right direction. In his case, at least, the epitaph on his gravestone is accurate: 'He was a loving husband and a loving father and a true friend.'

Sources

Most of the extracts from Trollope's novels and short stories come from narrative passages. Selections within quotation marks come from dialogue and do not necessarily represent Trollope's own views. Titles of short stories are in quotation marks, those of books are italicised. Page numbers are given where there is only one edition; otherwise chapter numbers or titles are used. As there are two editions of his letters, only the date is given. Publication details can be found in my biography, *Anthony Trollope: A Victorian in His World* (Duckworth, 1990) or in Michael Sadleir, *Trollope: A Bibliography*.

To be Anthony Trollope

I have certainly always had also before my eyes the charms of reputation ... I wished from the beginning to be something more than a clerk in the Post Office. To be known as somebody, to be Anthony Trollope if it be no more, is to me much. The feeling is a very general one, and I think beneficent ... The infirmity is so human that the man who lacks it is either above or below humanity. I own to the infirmity.   *Autobiography*, VI

I am simply known to you as being one who has helped by his writings to amuse the age in which he lives.
                    Speech at the Liverpool Institute, 1873

I have written above 80 novels and novelettes, have written about almost all English speaking people, have written a life of Cicero, and memoirs of Caesar and Thackeray. I have also been twice round the world, and was for 35 years in the Post Office ... The articles about my works have never been important, nor need they be.
                                        Letter, 29 Nov. 1881
[Trollope wrote 47 novels and several volumes of short stories.]

I remember well, when I was still the junior boy in the school, Dr Butler, the headmaster, stopping me in the street, and asking me ... whether it was possible that Harrow School was disgraced by so disreputably dirty a little boy as I! Oh, what I felt at that moment! ... I do not doubt that I was dirty; but I think he was cruel. He must have known me ... for he was in the habit of flogging me constantly. Perhaps he did not recognise me by my face.
                    Autobiography, I

[Trollope at a dinner party at George Eliot's house]: 'I sit down every morning at 5:30 with my watch on my desk, and for three hours I regularly produce 250 words every quarter of an hour' ... 'There are days and days together,' she groaned out, 'when I cannot write a line.' 'Yes!' said

Trollope, 'with imaginative work like yours that is quite natural; but with my mechanical stuff it's a sheer matter of industry. It's not the head that does it – it's the cobbler's wax on the seat and the sticking to my chair!'

Frederic Harrison, *Studies in Early Victorian Literature*, 220-3

I finished on Thursday the novel I was writing, and on Friday I began another. Nothing really frightens me but the idea of enforced idleness. As long as I can write books even though they be not published, I think that I can be happy.

Letter, 21 Dec. 1880

[A lady at a dinner party]: 'Do you believe, Mr Trollope, in inherited genius?' Before turning to answer her question, he whispered to me, 'I believe much more in cobbler's wax.'　　　　　*Graphic*, 23 Dec. 1882

[On a visit to an Observatory in South Africa, the director asked Trollope, 'Do you care for stars?']: I care only for men and women.　　　　　*South Africa*, 'Capetown'

I do not think it probable that my name will remain among those who in the next century will be known as the writers of English prose fiction.　　　　　*Autobiography*, XX

A demonstrative person … is he who is desirous of speaking out what is in his heart. For myself I am inclined to think that such speaking out has its good ends … What is in a man, let it come out and be known to those around him; if it be bad it will find correction; if it be good it will spread and be beneficient.

Castle Richmond, XXXII

I have lived with my characters, and thence has come whatever success I have attained.

Autobiography, XII

In the Post Office it was my principle always to obey authority in everything instantly, but never to allow my mouth to be closed as to the expression of my opinion.

Autobiography, VIII

[To another postal official]: I differ from you entirely! What was it you said?

Edmund Yates, *Recollections & Experiences*, I.392-5

I think it very natural that men should have a bias in their minds.

Before Parliamentary Committee,
Parliamentary Papers, 1854-5, XI

I do not like photographs, and dislike my own worse than all others.

Letter, 15 Aug. 1878

[The concluding words of the Barsetshire novels]: To me Barset has been a real county, and its city a real city, and the spires and towers have been before my eyes, and the voices of the people are known to my ears, and the pavement of the city ways are familar to my footsteps … I have been induced to wander among them too long by my love of old friendships, and by the sweetness of old faces.

Last Chronicle of Barset, LXXXIV

Religion, the Church & the Clergy

Christ came to us, and we do not need another teacher.

Cicero, I.66

The two doctrines which seem to mark most clearly the difference between the men whom we regard, the one as a pagan and the other as a Christian, are the belief in a future life and the duty of doing well by our neighbours. *Ibid.*

To threaten [eternal damnation] while the life is in the man is human. To believe in the execution of those threats when the life has passed away is almost beyond the power of humanity.

'The Spotted Dog'

It is when things go badly with us here, and for most of us only then, that we think that we can see through the dark clouds into the joys of heaven.

He Knew He Was Right, LXXIII

There are women ... who think that the acerbities of religion are intended altogether for their own sex.

Linda Tressel, I

We cannot rest on religion merely by saying we will do so.

Thackeray, 135

Alas! how many of us from week to week call ourselves worms and dust and miserable sinners ... and yet in all our doings before the world cannot bring home to ourselves the conviction that we require other guidance than our own.

Three Clerks, IX

Who amongst us have not made ... some resolve ... at the sound of the preacher's voice – and forgotten it before our foot was well over the threshold?

Bertrams, VII

You can sit still on a Sunday morning, in the cold, on a very narrow bench, with no comfort appertaining, and listen for half an hour to a rapid outflow of words, which, for any purpose of instruction or edification, are absolutely useless to you ... Try to undergo the same thing in your own house on a Wednesday afternoon, and see where you will be.

Miss Mackenzie, VIII

I will believe no man who tells me that he would not sooner earn two loaves than one; and if two, then two hundred ... The preachers have preached well, but on this matter they have preached in vain ... All men who work desire to prosper by their work, and they so desire by the nature given to them by God. Wealth and progress must go hand in hand together.

North America, I.xiv

'Tis in this way that the truth of that awful mystery, the fall of man, comes home to us; that we cannot hear the devil plead, and resist the charm of his eloquence. To listen is to be lost.

Three Clerks, IX

[After enduring a political sermon]: One hardly knows where the affairs of this world end, or where those of the next begin ... [Were] the holy men ... doing stage-work or church-work?   *North America*, I.xix

God is good to us, and heals those wounds with a rapidity which seems to us impossible when we look forward, but which is regarded with very insufficient wonder when we look backward.   *Bertrams*, III

I judge a man by his actions with men, much more than his declarations Godwards.   Letter, 8 June 1876

It is very hard to come at the actual belief of any man. Indeed how should we hope to do so when we find it so very hard to come at our own.

Pall Mall Gazette, 25 Jan. 1866

I do not prize humility before God. To my God I can be but true, and if I think myself to have done well I cannot but say so ... how can I be humble before God when I tell him that I expect from him eternal bliss as the reward of my life here on earth.   Letter, 8 June 1876

Whatever our Sundays be, let them be a comfort to us ... Unless our day of worship be a comfort, our worship will avail us but little.   *New Zealander*, 92

The ordinary life of gentlefolk in England does not admit of direct clerical interference.   *John Caldigate*, XXXII

[The literal interpretation of the Bible]: If one could really believe that the old shore is best, who would leave it? Who would not wish to be secure if he knew where security lay? ... With hands outstretched towards the old places, with sorrowing hearts, with hearts which still love the old teachings which the mind will no longer accept, we ... go out in our little boats, and search for a land that will be new to us ... Who would not stay behind if it were possible to him?   *Pall Mall Gazette*, 25 Jan. 1866

Infidelity that can make itself successful will, at any rate, bring an income.   *Bertrams*, XVIII

No one becomes an infidel at once. A man who has really believed does not lose by a sudden blow the firm convictions of his soul. But when the work has been once commenced, when the first step has been taken, the pace becomes frightfully fast.   *Bertrams*, XXVI

There come upon us all as we grow up in years, hours in which it is impossible to keep down the conviction that everything is vanity … It is the presence of thoughts such as these that needs the assurance of a heaven to save the thinker from madness or from suicide. It is when the feeling of this pervading vanity is strongest on him, that he who doubts of heaven most regrets his incapacity for belief.   *Ralph the Heir*, LI

Religious consolation is the best cure for all griefs; but it must not be looked for specially with regard to any individual sorrow. A religious man, should he become bankrupt … will find true consolation in his religion … But a bankrupt, who has not thought much of such things, will hardly find solace by taking up religion for that special occasion.   'Courtship of Susan Bell'

[During an after-dinner discussion on immortality]: If I thought I should never see dear old Thackeray again, I should be a very unhappy man.
                Charles Tuckerman, *Personal Recollections*, II.8-11

The apostle of Christianity and the infidel can meet without a chance of a quarrel; but it is never safe to bring together two men who differ about a saint or a surplice.
                              Phineas Redux, XXXIII

But no lesson is truer than that which teaches us to believe that God does temper the wind to the shorn lamb. To how many has it not seemed, at some one period of their lives, that all was over for them … And yet they have lived to laugh again, to feel that the air was warm and the earth fair, and that God in giving them ever-springing hope has given everything.   *Orley Farm*, LXXIX

I believe that the reputed sinners are much more numerous than the sinners.

The Small House at Allington, XLIII

[The difference between the Christian and the Mohamme-dan is that the latter] does not see the difference between good and evil as we see it. That which is good to us is evil to him, and that which is most evil to us, such as tyranny, cruelty, and oppression, are all absolutely good to him.

Speech at St James's Hall, 1876

How much kinder is God to us than we are willing to be to ourselves! At the loss of every dear face, at the last going of every well beloved one, we all doom ourselves to an eternity of sorrow, and look to waste ourselves away in an ever-running fountain of tears. How seldom does such grief endure! how blessed is the goodness which forbids it to be so! *Barchester Towers*, II

'How did the synod go on?' 'The synod made an ass of itself; as synods always do. It is necessary to get a lot of men together, for the show of the thing, otherwise the world will not believe.' *Claverings*, XXXII

[Of an Evangelical clergyman]: He was a devout, good man … sincere, hard-working, sufficiently intelligent … but deficient in one vital qualification for a clergyman of the Church of England; he was not a gentleman. May I not call it a necessary qualification for a clergyman of any church? … I am by no means prepared to define what I do mean, thinking, however, that most men and most women will understand me. *Rachel Ray*, VI

A dean has been described as a church dignitary who … has little to do and a good deal to get.

Pall Mall Gazette, 2 December 1865

Praying is by no means the easiest work … Kneeling is easy; the repetition of the well-known word is easy; the putting on of some solemnity of mind is perhaps not difficult. But to remember what you are asking, why you are asking, of whom you are asking; to feel sure that you want what you do ask, and that this asking is the best way to get it; that on the whole is not easy. *Bertrams*, XXVI

The church was large and straggling and ill-arranged, and on this particular Sunday had been almost empty … 'Does that gentleman generally draw large congregations?' asked the persistent Senator. 'We don't go in for drawing congregations here … We have a church in every parish for those who choose to attend it.' *American Senator*, XII

[The Bishop] was beautiful and decorous in his gait of manner, as it behooves a clergyman of the Church of England to be. *Dr Wortle's School*, XI

Clergymen who preach sermons against the love of money … know that the love of money is so distinctive a characteristic of humanity that such sermons are mere platitudes called for by customary but unintelligent piety. All material progress has come from man's desire to do the best he can for himself and those about him, and civilisation and Christianity itself have been made possible by such progress. *Autobiography*, VI

It has been hard to steer between idolatry and irreverence, between too much ceremony and too little. We, with our much maligned church in England, may perhaps boast that we have done so. *Cornhill Magazine*, November 1862

No man reverences a clergyman, as a clergyman, so slightly as a brother clergyman.

Last Chronicle of Barset, V

[On the Evangelical view of life as a 'vale of tears']: Then why has the world been made so pleasant? Why is the fruit of the earth so sweet; and the trees, why are they so green; and the mountains so full of glory? Why are women so lovely? and why is it that the activity of man's mind is the only sure forerunner of man's progress?

Belton Estate, VII

'Those are the sort of men [said Archdeacon Grantly] who will ruin the Church of England … It is not the dissenters or the papists that we should fear, but the set of canting, low-bred hypocrites who are wriggling their way in among us: men who have no fixed principle, no standard ideas of religion or doctrine, but who take up some popular cry.'

Barchester Towers, VI

'When one reflects what a deal of harm a bishop may do, one wishes that there was some surer way of getting bishops.'   *Eustace Diamonds*, LIII

I trust … I shall not be thought to scoff at the pulpit, though some may imagine that I do not feel all the reverence that is due to the cloth. I may question the infallibility of the teachers, but I hope that I shall not therefore be accused of doubt as to the thing to be taught.

Barchester Towers, VI

Clergymen are like women. As long as they're pure, they're a long sight purer than other men; but when they fall, they sink deeper.   *Miss Mackenzie*, XXIV

'If you had been led by me, Archdeacon, you would never have put a bachelor into St. Ewold's.' 'But, my dear, you don't mean to say that all bachelor clergymen misbehave themselves.' 'I don't know that clergymen are so much better than other men,' said Mrs Grantly.

Barchester Towers, XLVII

An affectionate letter from a bishop must surely be the most disagreeable missive which a parish clergyman can receive. Affection from one man to another is not natural in letters. A bishop never writes affectionately unless he means to reprove severely.

Dr Wortle's School, XIV

[On a High Church lady]: She assumes a smile of gentle ridicule when the Archbishop of Canterbury is named.

Barchester Towers, LIII

For myself, I love the name of State and Church, and believe that much of our English well-being has depended on it. I have made up my mind to think that union good, and not to be turned away from that conviction. Nevertheless I am not prepared to argue the matter. One does not always carry one's proof at one's finger-ends.

North America, I.xix

Women, Love & Marriage

To the taste of any woman the enthusiasm of another
woman is never very palatable.   'Mrs General Talboys'

Had she been a man ... she might have been a prime
minister, or an archbishop ... Fortunately for us and for the
world ... the port of literature is open to women.
'Mrs Brumby'

The women of America have that strength of mind which
has been wanting to those of Europe. In the United States
woman will at last learn to exercise her proper mission.
'Unprotected Female at the Pyramids'

Had she not been so much the lady, she might have been
more the woman.   *Miss Mackenzie*, IX

'But the men-cooks are the best,' said Nora ... 'All the
things that women do, men do better.' 'There are two
things they can't do,' said Priscilla ... 'They can't suckle
babies, and they can't forget themselves.'
He Knew He Was Right, XXV

The tact of women excels the skill of men.
Claverings, XLI

A woman is always angry with the woman, who has
probably been quite passive, and rarely with the man, who
is ever the real transgressor.
He Knew He Was Right, LXXII

Girls are understood by their mothers better than they are
by their fathers.   *Ibid.*, LXXV

'What makes me sure that this fuss about making men and
women all the same must be wrong, is just the fact that
men can get along without women, and women can't
without men.'   *Eustace Diamonds*, XXIII

Female friendships are slower in their growth, for the
suspicion of women is perhaps stronger than that of men.
'Journey to Panama'

Remember this, there is no tyranny to a woman like telling
her of her duty.   *Phineas Finn*, LV

Women … are the nursing mothers of mankind, and in that
law their fate is written with all its joys and all its privileges
… The best right a woman has is the right to a husband,
and that is the right to which I would recommend every
young woman here and in the States.
North America, I.xviii

The little sacrifices of society are all made by women, as are
also the great sacrifices of life. A man who is good for
anything is always ready for his duty, and so is a good
woman always ready for a sacrifice.
Small House at Allington, XIII

The world is harder to women than to men … a woman
often loses much by the chance of adverse circumstances
which a man only loses by his own misconduct.
Belton Estate, XXI

Women … are accustomed to look deeper into men at the
first sight than other men will trouble themselves to do.
Phineas Finn, XI

You cannot by Act of Congress or Parliament make the
woman's arm as strong as the man's or deprive her of her
position as the bearer of children. We may trouble
ourselves much by debating a question which superior
power has settled for us … The necessity of the supremacy
of man is as certain to me as the eternity of the soul.
Letter, 4 Apr. 1879

For a true spirit of persecution one should always go to a
woman; and the milder, the sweeter, the more loving …
the stronger will be that spirit within her.
Rachel Ray, XXV

[On veiled Mohammedan women in the Holy Land]: The
female followers of the Prophet … No one could behold
them without wishing that the eclipse had been total.
Bertrams, IX

Women … are entitled to everything that chivalry can give
them. They should sit while men stand. They should be
served while men wait. Men should be silent when they
speak … There is a reason for this deference … A man will
serve a woman, will suffer for her … because she is weaker
than he and needs protection. Let her show herself to be as
strong … and the very idea of chivalry, though it may live
for a while by the strength of custom, must perish and die
out of men's hearts.   *Australia*, 'Victoria', VIII

He was … selfish in his love. Most men are so.
The Bertrams, XX

There are both men and women to whom even the delays
and disappointments of love are charming, even when
they exist to the detriment of hope.
Way We Live Now, VIII

Women of the class to which I allude [feminists] are always
talking of their rights; but seem to have a most indifferent
idea of their duties.   *North America*, I.xiv

Power and will are the gifts a woman most loves in a man.
Bertrams, XX

All the virtues in the calendar, though they exist on each
side, will not make a man and woman happy together,
unless there be sympathy.   *Phineas Finn*, XXIII

Some one has said that grief is half removed when it is
shared. How little that some one knew about it! Half
removed! When it is duly shared between two loving
hearts, does not love fly off with eight-tenths of it?
Bertrams, XLVI

Men are cowards before [in front of] women until they
become tyrants.   *Small House at Allington*, XIV

To see a man eat and drink, and wear his slippers, and sit at ease in his chair, is delightful to the feminine heart that loves. When I heard the other day that a girl had herself visited the room prepared for a man in her mother's house, then I knew that she loved him, though I had never before believed it.   *Phineas Redux*, XI

In matters of love men do not see clearly in their own affairs. They say that faint heart never won fair lady; and it is amazing to me how fair ladies are won, so faint are often men's hearts!   *Warden*, VII

Lust is ever bad, and love ever good. That I take to be a truth as arranged by God.

> Note written by Trollope in his copy of Bacon's *Essays*, next to the essay 'On Love'

It is very hard sometimes to know how intensely we are loved, and of what value our presence is to those who love us.   *Last Chronicle of Barset*, XLIX

The match-making of mothers is the natural result of mother's love; for the ambition of one woman for another is never other than this; that the one loved by her shall be given to a man to be loved more worthily.

Vicar of Bullhampton, LXVII

Love desires an equal.

Duke's Children, XXI

You should not laugh at those who have [married], for you don't know what you may come to yourself, when you're married.   *Framley Parsonage*, III

It is the man who has no peace at home that declares abroad that his wife is an angel.

Duke's Children, LXXI

What comfort does a woman get out of her husband unless she may be allowed to talk to him about everything?

Dr Wortle's School, IV

Long engagements are bad, no doubt. Everybody has always said so. But a long engagement may be better than none at all.   *Ibid.*, VIII

Man by instinct desires in his wife something softer, sweeter, more refined than himself.

Three Clerks, XXXI

Don't let any wife think that she will satisfy her husband by perfect obedience. Overmuch virtue in one's neighbours is never satisfactory to us sinners.

Bertrams, XXXIII

He was one of those men of whom it may be said that they have no possible claim to remain unmarried.

He Knew He Was Right, XXX

[A] wedding-breakfast ... is the worst of all feeding ... the profusion of champagne, not sometimes of the very best ... and then the speeches! They fall generally to the lot of some middle-aged gentlemen, who seem always to have been selected for their incapacity!

Mr Scarborough's Family, LIX

The full meaning of marriage can never be known by those who, at their first outspring into life, are surrounded by all that money can give.   *Bertrams*, XXX

For a man with sound [severe] views of domestic power and marital rights always choose a Radical!

Lady Anna, XLVI

For those who have managed that things shall run smoothly over the domestic rug there is no happier time of life than these long candlelight hours of home and silence. No spoken content or uttered satisfaction is necessary. The fact that [it] is felt is enough for peace.

Orley Farm, XXI

The theory of man and wife – that special theory in accordance with which the wife is to bend herself in loving submission before her husband – is very beautiful; and would be good altogether if it could only be arranged that the husband should be the stronger and the greater of the two … In ordinary marriages … the stronger and the greater takes the lead, whether clothed in petticoats or in … trousers.   *Belton Estate*, XI

This moulding of a wife had failed … as it always must fail.
                                                  Orley Farm, LIV

To neither man nor woman does the world fairly begin till seated together in their first mutual home … [after] the excitement of their honeymoon is over.

                                                  Bertrams, XXX

A wife does not cease to love her husband because he gets into trouble. She does not turn against him because others have quarrelled with him. She does not separate her lot from his because he is in debt! Those are the times when a wife, a true wife, sticks closest to her husband, and strives the hardest to lighten the weight of his cares by the tenderness of her love!   *Rachel Ray*, XX

No social question has been so important to us as that of the great bond of matrimony. And why? Because every most wholesome joy and most precious duty of our existence depends upon our inner family relations.
                      Lecture on 'English Prose Fiction', 1871

No pain or misery has as yet come to me since the day I was married; if any man should speak well of the married state, I should do so.   Letter, 7 Apr. 1861

Life

Nothing can be so deleterious to a people at large as a lax feeling in regard to general honesty.
                      Letter XV to the *Liverpool Mercury*, 1875

There is surely no greater mistake than to suppose that reverence is snobbishness. *Thackeray*, 86

'Tell 'ee what, Master Crawley; and yer reverence mustn't think as I means to be preaching; there ain't nowt a man can't bear if he'll only be dogged … It's dogged as does it. It ain't thinking about it.' *Last Chronicle of Barset*, LXI

Pluck [is] … that sort of hardihood which we may not quite call courage, but which in a world well provided with policemen is infinitely more useful than courage.
The American Senator, LXVII

His curates … threw off as far as they could that zeal which is so dear to the youthful mind but which so often seems to be weak and flabby to their elders.
Dr Wortle's School, I

I fancy that a policeman considers that every man in the street would be properly 'run in,' if only all the truth about the man had been known. *Thackeray*, 81

[Of fanatical opponents of fox hunting]: 'Philanimalists … a small knot of self-anxious people who think they possess among them all the bowels [feelings] of the world … the ladies and gentlemen to whom I allude, not looking very clearly … put their splay feet down now upon this ordinary operation and now upon that, and call upon the world to curse the cruelty of those who will not agree with them.'
American Senator, LXXIII

That which enables the avaricious and the unjust to pass scatheless through the world is not the ignorance of the world as to their sins, but the indifference of the world whether they be sinful or no. *Bertrams*, XXIX

That feeling of over-due bills, of bills coming due, of accounts overdrawn, of tradesmen unpaid, of general money cares, is very dreadful at first; but it is astonishing how soon men get used to it. A load which would crush a man at first becomes, by habit, not only endurable, but easy and comfortable to the bearer.
Framley Parsonage, XII

We do not scruple to attribute to those who are indifferent some inferiority of intelligence. *Thackeray*, 191

For the ordinary purposes of conversation a superficial knowledge of many things goes further than an intimacy with one or two. 'Turkish Bath'

If there be an existence of wretchedness on earth it must be that of the elderly, worn-out roué.

Framley Parsonage, XII

I have usually found warnings to be of no avail, and often to be ill-founded ... No one ever attempted to gouge me in Kentucky or draw a revolver on me in California. I have lived in Paris as cheaply as elsewhere; and have invariably found Jews to be more liberal [i.e. generous] than other men. *South Africa*, 'Introduction'

The word that is written is a thing capable of permanent life, and lives frequently to the confusion of its parent. A man should make his confessions always by word of mouth if it be possible. *Claverings*, XLII

A man when he wishes to use burning words should use them while the words are on fire.

Old Man's Love, IX

If you want to ascertain the inner ways or habits of life of any man, woman, or child, see ... his or her bedroom.
North America, I.xvii

Whatever be the misery to be endured, get it over. The horror of every agony is in its anticipation.
Way We Live Now, XXXIX

Heaven defend me from angry letters! ... This at least should be a rule through the letter-writing world: that no angry letter be posted till four-and-twenty hours shall have elapsed since it was written ... Sit down and write your letter; write it with all the venom in your power; spit out your spleen at the fullest; 'twill do you good ... say all that you can say with all your poisoned eloquence, and gratify yourself by reading it while your temper is still hot. Then put it in your desk; and, as a matter of course, burn it before breakfast the following morning. Believe me that you will then have a double gratification.

Bertrams, XVIII

No one thinks of defending himself to a newspaper except an ass. *Small House at Allington*, XXXVI

Let the truth of the evil be told, and the truth will always deter, deter from vice. *St Pauls*, Oct. 1869

Fortune favours the brave; and the world certainly gives the most credit to those who are able to give an unlimited credit to themselves. *Bertrams*, XXXV

That I, or any man, should tell everything of himself, I hold to be impossible. *Autobiography*, I

A man, when he undertakes to advise another, should not be down in the mouth himself. *Landleaguers*, XL

It is very well to have friends to lean upon, but it is not always well to lean upon one's friends.

Orley Farm, LI

A man who desires to soften another man's heart, should always abuse himself. In softening a woman's heart, he should abuse her. *Last Chronicle of Barset*, XLIV

[Madame Max Goesler]: 'Remember, I do not recommend motion at all. Repose is my idea of life; repose and grapes.'
Phineas Finn, LX

The first impression which a parent should fix on the mind of a child is I think love of order. [It] is the reins by which all virtues are kept in their proper places and the vices, with whom the virtues run in one team, are controlled.
Entry in Trollope's youthful Commonplace Book

Last days are wretched days; and so are last moments wretched moments. It is not the fact that the parting is coming which makes these days and moments so wretched, but the feeling that something special is expected from them.

Small House at Allington, XV

Wise people, when they are in the wrong, always put themselves right by finding fault with the people against whom they have sinned. *Barchester Towers*, XXXVII

Writing, Novels & Reading

I hold that gentleman to be the best dressed whose dress no one observes. I am not sure but that the same may be said of an author's written language.

Thackeray, 200

In these days [we are] somewhat afraid of good broad English. *Framley Parsonage*, XII

Three hours a day will produce as much as a man ought to write.

Autobiography, XV

Of a magazine editor it is required that he should be patient, scrupulous, judicious, but above all things hard-hearted. *Thackeray*, 54

There is no way of writing well and also of writing easily.
Barchester Towers, XX

Literature … is a business which has its allurements. It requires no capital, no special education, no training, and may be taken up at any time without a moment's delay. If a man can command a table, a chair, pen, paper, and ink, he can commence his trade as literary man.

Thackeray, 10

He [the would-be author] had surrounded himself with his papers, had gotten his books together and read up his old notes, had planned chapters … revelled in those paraphernalia of work which are so dear to would-be working men; and then nothing had come of it.

Ralph the Heir, LI

Fancy [imagination] is a gift which the owner of it cannot measure, and the power of which, when he is using it, he cannot himself understand.   *Thackeray*, 24

I am well aware that there are many who think that an author ... should not regard money ... They who preach this doctrine ... require the practice of a so-called virtue which is contrary to nature ... Brains that are unbought will never serve the public much. Take away from English authors their copyrights, and you would very soon take away also from England her authors.

Autobiography, VI

Forethought is the elbow-grease which a novelist, or poet, or dramatist, requires.   *Thackeray*, 122

It would not suffice ... to scrape together a few facts, to indulge in some fiction, to tell a few anecdotes, and then to call his book a biography.

Ralph the Heir, XL

To think of a story is much harder work than to write it.

Thackeray, 123

A pleasant letter I hold to be the pleasantest thing that this world has to give. It should be good-humoured; witty it may be, but with a gentle diluted wit. Concocted brilliancy will spoil it altogether. Not long, so that it be tedious in the reading; nor brief, so that the delight suffice not to make itself felt ... It should never flatter. Flattery is always obvious. But underneath the visible stream of pungent water there may be the slightest undercurrent of eulogy, so that it be not seen, but only understood.

Bertrams, XVIII

[To a publisher who asked him to cut a short story]: Did you ever buy your own meat? That cutting down of 30 pages to 20, is what you proposed to the butcher when you asked him to take off the bony bit at this end, and the skinny bit at the other ... the butcher told you that nature had produced the joint bone and skin as you saw it.

Letter, 9 Aug. 1860

[Writing] is an art which no one teaches ... [That you] should be able to read and write is presumed, and that only.   *Thackeray*, 11

[Of George Eliot]: In truth she was one whose private life should be left in privacy, as may be said of all who have achieved fame by literary merits.

Letter, 17 Jan. 1881

There are men who never dream of a great work [book] ... But the men are many ... who adopt the task, who promise themselves the triumph, and then never struggle at all. The task is never abandoned; but days go by and weeks; and then months and years, and nothing is done. The dream of youth becomes the doubt of middle life, and then the despair of age.   *Ralph the Heir*, XL

[Victorian writers] rarely give ourselves time for condensation.   *Caesar*, 24

Literature happens to be the only occupation in which wages are not given in proportion to the goodness of the work done.

Speech on 10 Apr. 1869, St George's Hall, Liverpool,
for Dickens's Farewell Tour

Though readers prefer, or pretend to prefer, the romantic to the common in their novels ... yet I find that the absurd, the ludicrous, and even the evil, leave more impression behind them than the grand, the beautiful, or even the good.   *Thackeray*, 98

Do you not think that an author is in exactly the same category as any other workman, who has it on his conscience to use his life for doing good work for the world around him and who cannot do that good work unless he is paid for it?

Speaking as a member of the Royal Commission on Copyright
to a witness who said he would be 'sorry' to hear that great
authors wrote for money

No doubt many a literary artist so conceals his art that readers do not know that there is much art. But they like the books and read them, not knowing why.

Letter, 19 Nov. 1877

An author can hardly hope to be popular unless he can use popular language ... But all this must be learned and acquired, not while he is writing ... but long before. His language must come from him as music comes from the rapid touch of the great performer's fingers ... A man who thinks much of his words as he writes them will generally leave behind him work that smells of [hair] oil.

Autobiography, IX

[To a girl who was amazed that Dickens remembered her comments about a novel]: Authors never forget those who admire their works.

Laura Friswell, *In The Sixties & Seventies*, 169-70

Editors of newspapers are self-willed, arrogant, and stiff-necked, a race of men who believe much in themselves and little in anything else, with no feelings of reverence or respect for matters which are august enough to other men.

Phineas Redux, XXVII

The habit of writing clearly soon comes to the writer who is a severe critic to himself.   *Autobiography*, XII

Perhaps no terms have been so injurious to the profession of the novelist as those two words, hero and heroine.

Claverings, XXVIII

Barchester Towers was written before you were born. Of course I forget every word of it! But I don't. There is not a passage in it I do not remember. I always have to pretend to forget when people talk to me about my own old books. It looks modest ... But the writer never forgets.

Letter, 5 Dec. 1881

Men as I see them [in novels] are not often heroic.

Claverings, XXVIII

The true picture of life as it is, if it could be adequately painted, would show men what they are, and how they might rise, not, indeed, to perfection, but one step first, and then another on the ladder.

Eustace Diamonds, XXXV

Newspaper editors sport daily with the names of men of whom they do not hesitate to publish almost the severest words that can be uttered; but let an editor be himself attacked, even without his name, and he thinks that the thunderbolt of heaven should fall upon the offender.

Phineas Redux, XXVII

We who write fiction have taught purity of life, nobility of action, and self-denial and have taught those lessons with allurements to both the old and the young which no other teacher of the present day can reach, and which no prophet can teach.

Speech at the Royal Dramatic College, 1874

'Why *did* you let Crosbie jilt Lily Dale?', I asked Anthony Trollope one day. 'Why did I "let" him?', he repeated. 'How could I help it? He *would* do it, confound him!'

Contemporary Review, Aug. 1894

Leave-takings in novels are as disagreeable as they are in real life … What novelist … can impart an interest to the last chapter of his fictitious history? … Do I not myself know that I am at this moment in want of a dozen pages, and that I am sick with cudgelling my brains to find them?

Barchester Towers, LI

To base your life on the reading of novels, to make that the chief work of the mind and the intellect which God has given you; surely that must be very bad! Do you think that such an employment can be compatible with anything worthy of the name of higher education?

Lecture 'On the Higher Education of Women', 1867

The end of a novel, like the end of a children's dinner-party, must be made up of sweetmeats and sugar-plums.   *Barchester Towers*, LIII

Marriage [is] … the proper ending for a novel, the only ending, as this writer takes it to be.

Ayala's Angel, LXIV

The sorrows of our heroes and heroines, they are your delight, oh public! their sorrows, or their sins, or their absurdities; not their virtues, good sense, and consequent rewards.   *Barchester Towers*, LI

Perhaps the method of rushing at once 'in medias res' is, of all the ways of beginning a story … the least objectionable. The reader is made to think the gold lies so near the surface that he will be required to take very little trouble in digging for it.   *Duke's Children*, IX

At different periods in our history, the preacher, the dramatist, the essayist, and the poet have been efficacious over others … Now it is the novelist. There are reasons why we would wish it were otherwise. The reading of novels can hardly strengthen the intelligence.

Nineteenth Century, Jan. 1879

A novel should give a picture of common life enlivened by humour and sweetened by pathos … To my thinking, the plot is but the vehicle … when you have the vehicle without the passengers, a story of mystery in which the agents never spring to life, you have but a wooden show.

Autobiography, VII

Works of imagination are the sermons of the present day.
Speech at the Liverpool Institute, 1873

Dialogue is generally the most agreeable part of a novel.
Autobiography, XII

I hold it to be a convincing sign of a good novel that it takes long in the reading – that the reader finds that with due attention to the story he can hardly skip.
Note written by Trollope in his copy of Scott's *Old Mortality*

[The novelist's moral duty is to] teach ladies to be women and men to be gentlemen.   Speech at Royal Literary Fund

The novelist may not be dull. If he commit that fault, he can do neither harm nor good ... The writer of stories must please, or he will be nothing. And he must teach, whether he wish to teach or not.

Nineteenth Century, Jan. 1879

[On the tendency toward 'speculation' in American fiction]: On our side of the water we deal more with beef and ale and less with dreams.

North American Review, Sept. 1879

When I sit down to write a novel I do not at all know, and I do not very much care, how it is to end.

Autobiography, XIII

If a man have not acquired the habit of reading till he be old, he shall sooner in his old age learn to make shoes than learn the adequate use of a book.

Claverings, XLV

When the masses of English readers, in all English-reading countries, have agreed to love the writings of any writer, their verdict will be stronger than that of any one judge, let that judge be ever so learned and ever so thoughtful. However the writer may have achieved his object, he has accomplished that which must be the desire of every author, he has spoken to men and women who have opened their ears to his words, and have listened to them.

St Pauls, July 1870

General literature is perhaps the product which comes last from the energies of an established country. Men must eat before they can write, and all think of eating before they think of writing. Leisure ... is necessary for the production of books.

Australia, 'Victoria', IX

Literary merit will hardly set a magazine afloat, though when afloat it will sustain it.

Autobiography, XV

I regard the literature of a country as its highest produce, believing it to be more powerful in its general effect, and more beneficial in its results, than either statesmanship, professional ability, religious teaching, or commerce ... Literature is the child of leisure and wealth.

North America, II.xv

That I can read and be happy while I am reading, is a great blessing. Could I have remembered, as some men do, what I read, I should have been able to call myself an educated man … Something is always left, something dim and inaccurate, but still something sufficient to preserve the taste for more. I am inclined to think that it is so with most readers.   *Autobiography*, XX

Life [is] limited … there are some branches of human knowledge which must be renounced by anyone who values his brain.
                    Pall Mall Gazette, 17 Sept. 1880

Only those who have done it know how great is the labour of moving and arranging a few thousand volumes.
                    Autobiography, XX

Books are live things. Each has, and … loves its peculiar nook.   *Pall Mall Gazette*, 17 Sept. 1880

Literary criticism has in the present day become a profession, but it has ceased to be an art.
                    Autobiography, XIV

When young people begin their world of reading there is nothing so pleasant to them as knowing the little secrets of literature; who wrote this and that … [and who] puts the salt and pepper into those reviews.
                    Orley Farm, LVIII

The central character with Dickens had always been made beautiful with unnatural virtue.   *Thackeray*, 26

[George Eliot] is sometimes heavy – sometimes abstruse, sometimes almost dull, but always like an egg, full of meat.
                    Letter, 18 Sept. 1874

[Shakespeare was] definitely beyond his age in discovering the manliness of decency.
                    Note by Trollope in his copy of Beaumont and Fletcher

Cicero and Ovid have told us that to literature only could they look for consolation in their banishment. But then they speak of a remedy for sorrow, not a source of joy. No young man should dare to neglect literature. At some period of his life he will surely need consolation. And he may be certain that should he live to be an old man, there will be none other; except religion.

Duke's Children, XXV

By the common consent of all mankind who have read, poetry takes the highest place in literature.

Autobiography, XII

Politics

How seldom is it that theories stand the wear and tear of practice! *Thackeray*, 52

Let the toryism of the Tory be ever so strong, it is his destiny to carry out the purposes of his opponents.

'Why Frau Frohmann Raised Her Prices'

I have sometimes thought that there is no being so venomous, so bloodthirsty as a professed philanthropist.

North America, I.xvi

'In politics one should always look forward,' he said, as he held up to the light the glass of old port which he was about to sip; 'in real life it is better to look back, if one has anything to look back at.' *Bertrams*, XVI

I have hardly as yet met two Englishmen who were agreed as to the political power of the Sovereign.

American Senator, LXXVII

To him it certainly seemed that everything that was, was bad … But this is so usually the state of mind of all parliamentary critics.

He Knew He Was Right, LXVIII

If there is to remain among us a sovereign, that sovereign, even though divested of political power, should be endowed with all that personal respect can give. If we wish ourselves to be high, we should treat that which is over us as high.   *Thackeray*, 46-7

When we hear that a people have declared their intention of being better than their neighbours, and going upon a new theory that shall lead them direct to a terrestrial paradise, we button up our pockets and lock up our spoons.   *North America*, I.xix

There are certain things of which opposition members of Parliament complain loudly; and there are certain other things as to which they are silent. The line between these things is well known.

He Knew He Was Right, LXVIII

I utterly disbelieve in statistics as a science and am never myself guided by any long-winded statement of figures from a Chancellor of the Exchequer or such-like big-wig … Figures when they go beyond six in number, represent to me not facts, but dreams, or sometimes worse than dreams.

West Indies, 110

'And it is so comfortable to have theories that one is not bound to carry out,' said Phineas.   *Phineas Finn*, XL

To me it seems that no form of government that ever did exist, gives or has given so large a measure of individual freedom to all who live under it as a constitutional monarchy.   *North America*, I.vi

[Of the radical politician]: Having nothing to construct, he could always deal with generalities. Being free from responsibility, he was not called upon either to study details or to master even great facts. It was his business to inveigh against existing evils, and perhaps there is no easier business when once the privilege of an audience has been attained. It was his work to cut down forest-trees, and he had nothing to do with subsequent cultivation of the land.   *Phineas Finn*, XVIII

There is nothing more tyrannical than a strong popular feeling among a democratic people.

North America, I.xi

The Utopian politician travels as far as he can away from the despotism of patriarchal rule, but he travels in a circle and comes back to it.

Australia, 'South Australia', V

[Equality] ... is a doctrine to be forgiven when he who preaches it is ... striving to raise others to his own level; though utterly unpardonable when the preacher would pull down others to his level.

North America, II.iv

What good government ever was not stingy?

South Africa, 'Capetown'

No reform, no innovation ... stinks so foully in the nostrils of an English Tory politician as to be absolutely irreconcilable to him. When taken in the refreshing waters of office any such pill can be swallowed.

Bertrams, XVI

Men when they are canvassing never dine; and not often after they're elected.

Ralph the Heir, XXIII

Make all men equal today, and God has so created them that they shall be all unequal tomorrow.

Autobiography, XVI

In speaking, grand words come so easily, while thoughts, even little thoughts, flow so slowly!

Ralph the Heir, XVI

To practical Englishmen most of these international congresses seem to arrive at nothing ... Men will not be talked out of the convictions of their lives.

Orley Farm, XVII

A man to be useful in Parliament, must be able to confine himself and conform himself, to be satisfied with doing a little bit of a little thing at a time.

Autobiography, XVI

As years have rolled on, the strong have swallowed the weak, one strong man having eaten up half-a-dozen weak men ... The strong squire becomes a baronet and a lord, till he lords it a little too much, and a Manchester warehouseman buys him out. The strength of the country probably lies in the fact that the change is ever being made, but is never made suddenly.

Ralph the Heir, XLIX

I consider myself to be an advanced, but still a conservative Liberal.   *Autobiography*, XVI

He was gifted with that peculiar power which enables a man to have the last word in every encounter ... In a debate, the man of moderate parts will seem to be greater than the man of genius. But this skill of tongue, this glibness of speech is hardly an affair of intellect at all. It is, as is style to the writer, not the wares which he has to take to market, but the vehicle in which they may be carried. Of what avail to you is it to have filled granaries with corn if you cannot get your corn to the consumer?

Duke's Children, XXVI

A man who entertains in his mind any political doctrine, except as a means of improving the condition of his fellows, I regard as a political intriguer, a charlatan, and a conjuror.   *Autobiography*, XVI

The fault which people find with him is this, that he is not practical. He won't take the world as he finds it. If he can mend it, well and good; we all ought to do something to mend it; but while we are mending it we must live in it.

Orley Farm, LVIII

[Of candidates canvassing during an election]: Perhaps nothing more disagreeable, more squalid, more revolting to the senses, more opposed to personal dignity, can be conceived. The same words have to be repeated over and over again in the cottages, hovels, and lodgings of poor men and women who only understand that ... they are to be flattered instead of being the flatterers.

Duke's Children, LV

Nobles doubtless add dignity to a nation, and a country
can hardly stand high without dignity.

> Note written by Trollope in his copy of Bacon's *Essays*,
> next to that on 'Nobility'

There is always this danger in Mr Gladstone's oratory, that
he finds it easy to prove anything, and is therefore prone
to prove too much. *St Pauls*, Mar. 1870

[Political life]: The hatreds which sound so real when you
read the mere words, which look so true when you see
their scornful attitudes, on which for the time you are
inclined to pin your faith so implicitly, amount to nothing.

> *Landleaguers*, XLII

Of all the studies to which men and women can attach
themselves, that of politics is the first and foremost.

> Editorial for first issue of *St Pauls*, Oct. 1867

That exquisite combination of conservatism and progress
… [is England's] present strength and best security for the
future.

> *Can You Forgive Her?* XXIV

I do not much mind what a man's politics are, so that he
has got politics. So that he will concern himself with the
public welfare of his country and his race.

> Lecture, 'The Civil Service as a Profession', 1861

But in truth the capacity of a man … [to be Prime Minister]
does not depend on any power of intellect, or of
indomitable courage, or far-seeing cunning. The man is
competent simply because he is believed to be so.

> *Lord Palmerston*, 150

Briton[s] who take a delight in politics … should not be
desirous of peeping behind the scenes. No beholder at any
theatre should do so.

> *Can You Forgive Her?* XLII

There are many rocks which a young speaker in Parliament
should avoid, but no rock which requires such careful
avoiding as the rock of eloquence. *Ibid.*

The first necessity for good speaking is a large audience.
Phineas Finn, XVIII

A man destined to sit conspicuously on our Treasury bench, or on a seat opposite, should ask the Gods for a thick skin as a first gift.
Phineas Redux, XXXIII

Statesmen sitting together in a cabinet may resolve that they will set the world right by eloquence and benevolence combined; but the practices to which the world have been brought by long experience will avail more than eloquence and benevolence.
Landleaguers, XLI

He [Robespierre] believed in nothing but himself, and the reasoning faculty with which he felt himself to be endowed. He thought himself perfect … and wishing to make others perfect as he was, he fell into the lowest abyss of crime and misery … He seems almost to have been sent into the world to prove the inefficacy of human reason to effect human happiness.
La Vendée, XXII

With us regret is almost stronger than hope. We venerate old things because they are old.
Fortnightly Review, Aug. 1865

We hate an evil and we hate a change.
Pall Mall Gazette, 27 Nov. 1865

In almost every bosom there sits a parliament in which a conservative party is ever combating to maintain things old, while the liberal side of the house is always conquering, but its adversary is never conquered.
Fortnightly Review, Oct. 1865

[On the British Constitution]: 'It is liberty to growl about the iron fleet, or the ballot, or the taxes, or the peers, or the bishops, or anything else, except the House of Commons. That's the British Constitution.'
Phineas Finn, XX

He [J.S. Mill] who said that all Conservatives are stupid did not know them. Stupid Conservatives there may be, and there certainly are very stupid Radicals. The well-educated, widely-read Conservative, who is well assured that all good things are gradually being brought to an end by the voice of the people, is generally the pleasantest man to be met. *Eustace Diamonds*, IV

[After his 1872 visit to New Zealand]: Government cannot get the same work out of its workmen that is got by private employers. It cannot build a ship, or manage an estate, or erect a palace with that economy which a private master can ensure ... A profuse expenditure of government money in any community will taint the whole of it with the pervading sin. *Australia*, 'New Zealand'

Ireland

It has been my fate to have so close an intimacy with Ireland, that when I meet an Irishman abroad, I always recognise in him more of a kinsman than in an Englishman. *North America*, II.xvi

Where does one find girls so pretty, so easy, so sweet, so talkative as the Irish girls? And then with all their talking, and all their ease, who ever hears of their misbehaving? They certainly love flirting as they also love dancing. But they flirt without mischief and without malice.
'O'Conors of Castle Conor'

As a chance companion for a few idle minutes, is there any one so likely to prove himself agreeable as a well-informed, travelled Irishman? 'Turkish Bath'

Those provocative Irish tunes ... compel the hearers to dance whether they wish it or not. *Macdermots*, XIII

I should prefer the South to the North of Ireland, preferring on the whole papistical to presbyterian tendencies.

Letter, 23 Nov. 1854

The love which a poor Irishman feels for the gentleman whom he regards as his master ... is astonishing to an Englishman. I will not say that the feeling is altogether good. Love should come of love ... That unbounded respect for human grandeur cannot be altogether good; for human greatness, if the greatness be properly sifted, it may be so.

Castle Richmond, XXV

Ireland has been the vassal of England ... She was subjected to much ill-usage, and though she has readily accepted the language, the civilisation, and the customs of England, and has in fact grown rich by adopting them, the memories of former hardships have clung to her, and have made her ready to receive willingly the teachings of those whose only object it has been to undermine the prestige of the British Empire.

Landleaguers, XLI

[Of an Irish radical]: It was the battle, rather than the thing battled for, that was dear to him; the strife, rather than the result. He felt that it would be dull times in Dublin, when they should have no usurping Government to abuse, no Saxon Parliament to upbraid, no English laws to ridicule, and no Established Church to curse.

Kellys & O'Kellys, I

In Ireland staunch Protestantism consists too much in a hatred of Papistry – in that rather than in a hatred of those errors against which we Protestants are supposed to protest. Hence the cross – which should, I presume, be the emblem of salvation to us all – creates a feeling of dismay and often of disgust instead of love and reverence.

Castle Richmond, X

Human Nature

'I have meant to do right; but, Janet, it is so hard to do right.'   *Vicar of Bullhampton*, LXIV

We are always tempted to approve of that which we like, and to think that that which is good to us is good altogether … But that which is good and pleasant to us, is often not good and pleasant altogether.

North America, I.iv

Like all angry men, he loved his grievance.

Doctor Thorne, XII

I hold it natural that a man should wail to himself … And that which he says to himself he will say to his wife, if his wife be to him a second self.   *Cicero*, I.364

There is … no knowing the inside of another man's house, or reading the riddles of another man's joy and sorrow.

'Mrs General Talboys'

We are too apt to forget when we think of the sins and faults of men how keen may be their conscience in spite of their sins.   *Cousin Henry*, XVII

The English character, with its faults and virtues, its prejudices and steadfastness, can be better studied in the mansions of noblemen, in country-houses, in parsonages, in farms, and small meaningless towns, than in the great cities.   *Australia*, 'Victoria', VIII

A man with us will laugh at the Sir Johns and Sir Thomases who are seated around him, but still, when his time comes will be pleased that his wife shall be called 'My Lady.'

Cicero, II.105

When one is specially invited to be candid, one is naturally set upon one's guard ... When a man says to you, 'Let us be candid with each other,' you feel instinctively that he desires to squeeze you without giving a drop of water himself.   *Doctor Thorne*, XL

We, all of us, read more in the faces of those with whom we hold converse, than we are aware of doing. Of the truth, or want of truth in every word spoken to us, we judge, in great part, by the face of the speaker ... in nine cases out of ten our judgment is true. It is because our tenth judgment ... comes back upon us always with the effects of its error, that we teach ourselves to say that appearances cannot be trusted. If we did not trust them we should be walking ever in doubt, in darkness, and in ignorance.

Rachel Ray, XIX

Hope ... is of all our feelings the strongest.

Duke's Children, XXI

She had been so little thought of all her life by others, that she had never learned to think much of herself.

Kellys & O'Kellys, IV

Till we can become divine we must be content to be human, lest in our hurry for a change we sink to something lower.   *Barchester Towers*, XLIII

He had three days in which to make up his mind. It may be a question whether three days are ever much better than three minutes for such a purpose. A man's mind will very generally refuse to make itself up until it is driven and compelled by emergency. The three days are passed not in forming but in postponing judgment. In nothing is procrastination so tempting as in thought.

Ayala's Angel, XLI

All our motives are mixed.

Orley Farm, XVI

Nobody can, in truth, endure to be told of shortcomings, either on his own part or on that of his country. He himself can abuse himself, or his country; but he cannot endure it from alien lips.   *American Senator*, LI

No man after twenty-five can afford to call special attention to his coat, his hat, his cravat, or his trousers.

He Knew He Was Right, I

What is it that we all live upon but self-esteem? When we want praise it is only because praise enables us to think well of ourselves.

Ibid., XVI

There are few of us who have not allowed our thoughts to work on this or that villainy, arranging the method of its performance, though the performance itself is far enough from our purpose.

Ralph the Heir, XI

There is nothing in the world so difficult as that task of making up one's mind.

Phineas Finn, LX

There is nothing perhaps so generally consoling to a man as a well-established grievance; a feeling of having been injured, on which his mind can brood from hour to hour, allowing him to plead his own cause in his own court, within his own heart, and always to plead it successfully.

Orley Farm, VIII

Every man to himself is the centre of the whole world; the axle on which it all turns. All knowledge is but his own perception of the things around him.

Can You Forgive Her? XXXIX

We always want that which we can't get easily.

Orley Farm, LXVI

When one Esquimau meets another, do the two, as an invariable rule, ask after each other's health? Is it inherent in all human nature to make this obliging inquiry? Did any reader of this tale ever meet any … acquaintance without asking some such question, and did any one ever listen to the reply?

The Warden, XV

A self-imposed trouble will not allow itself to be banished.

Small House at Allington, XXVIII

The secrets of the world are very marvellous but they are not themselves half so wonderful as the way in which they become known to the world.

Phineas Redux, XL

They who do not understand that a man may be brought to hope that which of all things is the most grievous to him, have not observed with sufficient closeness the perversity of the human mind.

He Knew He Was Right, XXXVIII

That worst of all diseases, a low idea of humanity.

Eustace Diamonds, XXVIII

He half thought as he spoke, or thought that he thought so. Unless it be on subjects especially endeared to us the thoughts of but few of us go much beyond this.

He Knew He Was Right, XLVI

Brothers do not always care much for a brother's success, but a sister is generally sympathetic.

Eustace Diamonds, IV

The good and the bad mix themselves so thoroughly in our thoughts, even in our aspirations, that we must look for excellence rather in overcoming evil than in freeing ourselves from its influence.

He Knew He Was Right, LX

As man is never strong enough to take unmixed delight in good, so may we presume also that he cannot be quite so weak as to find perfect satisfaction in evil.

Eustace Diamonds, I

He had not that perfect faith in mankind which is the surest evidence of a simple mind.

Mr Scarborough's Family, XXXII

It is not the sorrows but the annoyances of life which impede ... These little lacerations of the spirit, not the deep wounds, make the difficulty [in thinking].

'Walk in a Wood'

We are told to love others as ourselves, and it is hard to do so. But I think that we never hate others, never despise others, as we are sometimes compelled by our own convictions and self-judgement to hate and despise ourselves. *Claverings*, XXI

Most men have got some little bit of pet tyranny in their hearts. *Mr Scarborough's Family*, XL

The most difficult thing that a man has to do is to think. 'Walk in a Wood'

Let any of us, in any attempt that we may make, convince ourselves with ever so much firmness that we shall fail, yet we are hardly the less down-hearted when the failure comes. We assure ourselves that we are not sanguine, but we assure ourselves falsely. It is man's privilege to be sanguine; his nature, and perhaps his greatest privilege. *Bertrams*, XXXII

We may almost say that a man is only as strong as his weakest moment. *Ralph the Heir*, XXVII

Nothing is so powerful in making a man selfish as misfortune. *Castle Richmond*, XXV

We are all apt to think when our days are dark that there is no darkness so dark as our own. *Bertrams*, XXXIII

It is ever so much easier to proffer kindness graciously than to receive it with grace.

Last Chronicle of Barset, L

The rising in life of our familiar friends is, perhaps, the bitterest morsel of the bitter bread which we are called upon to eat ... But we do eat it; and after a while it becomes food to us – when we find ourselves able to use, on behalf, perhaps, of our children, the influence of those whom we had once hoped to leave behind in the race of life.

Phineas Redux, XXXII

When men think much, they can rarely decide.

Sir Harry Hotspur, XX

People are so much more worldly in practice than they are
in theory, so much keener after their own gratification in
detail than they are in the abstract.

Last Chronicle of Barset, LVI

He did not find in the contemplation of his grievance all
that solace which a grievance usually gives.

Small House at Allington, XXXVIII

Women sympathise most effectually with men, as men do
with women.   *Phineas Finn*, LIV

Consolation from the world's deceit is very common.
Mothers obtain it from their children, and men from their
dogs. Some men even do so from their walking-sticks,
which is just as rational.

Barchester Towers, XLIV

He was a man who had long since resolved that his life
should be a success. It would seem that all men would so
resolve … But the majority of men, as I take it, make no
such resolution, and very many men resolve that they will
be unsuccessful.

Small House at Allington, XLV

With all of us, in the opinion which we form of those
around us, we take unconsciously the opinion of others. A
woman is handsome because the world says so. Music is
charming to us because it charms others. We drink our
wine with other men's palates, and look at our pictures
with other men's eyes.

Last Chronicle of Barset, LII

It is the view which the mind takes of a thing which creates
the sorrow that arises from it.

Small House at Allington, L

He was above, or rather below, all prejudices.

Barchester Towers, IX

It is well that some respect should be maintained from the
low in station towards those who are high, even when no
respect has been deserved.   *Claverings*, XLIV

There are men who have the most lively gratification in calling lords and marquises their friends, though they know that nobody believes a word of what they say ... It is a gentle insanity which prevails in the outer courts of every aristocracy; and as it brings with itself considerable annoyance and but a lukewarm pleasure, it should not be treated with too keen a severity.

Small House at Allington, LIX

Rumour, when she has contrived to sound the first note on her trumpet, soon makes a loud peal audible enough.

Barchester Towers, XLVII

[Newspapers]: Who is there that abstains from reading that which is printed in abuse of himself?

Phineas Finn, XLVII

Nothing makes a man so cross as success ... Your successful man eats too much and his stomach troubles him; he drinks too much and his nose becomes blue ... Success is the necessary misfortune of life, but it is only to the very unfortunate that it comes early.

Orley Farm, XLIX

Is it not a pity that people who are bright and clever should so often be exceedingly improper? and that those who are never improper should so often be dull and heavy?

Barchester Towers, XXXIII

It is very hard, that necessity of listening to a man who says nothing.   *Small House at Allington,* XII

There is nothing so prejudicial to a cause as temper. This man is declared to be unfit for any position of note, because he always shows temper.   *Phineas Redux,* IX

A man must be an idiot or else an angel, who after the age of forty shall attempt to be just to his neighbours.

Barchester Towers, XXXVII

If you, my reader, ever chanced to slip into the gutter on a wet day, did you not find that the sympathy of the bystanders was by far the severest part of your misfortune?

Small House at Allington, XXXI

There is perhaps no feeling stronger in the mind of man
than the desire to own a morsel of land.

Australia, 'Queensland', VIII

A man should not have his Christian name used by every
Tom and Dick without his sanction.   *American Senator*, I

The trouble in civilised life of entertaining company … is so
great that it cannot but be a matter of wonder that people
are so fond of attempting it.

Barchester Towers, XXXVI

A change of name implies such a confession of failure.

Is He Popenjoy? XVII

Out of the full heart the mouth speaks.

Australia, 'Victoria', VIII

A man who will plant a poplar, a willow, or even a
blue-gum in a treeless country – how good is he! But the
man who will plant an oak will surely feel the greenness of
its foliage and the pleasantness of its shade when he is
lying down, down beneath the sod!

South Africa, 'Western Province'

It is, I think, certainly the fact that women … are less
shocked by dishonesty [than men] … Where is the woman
who thinks it wrong to smuggle?

Miss Mackenzie, X

It is through great cities that the civilisation of the world
has progressed, and the charms of life been advanced. Man
in his rudest state begins in the country, and in his most
finished state may retire there. But the battle of the world
has to be fought in the cities.

North America, I.iv

Young Men

That terrible habit which prevails among bachelors, of allowing his work to remain ever open, never finished, always confused, with papers above books, and books above papers, looking as though no useful product could ever be made to come forth from such chaotic elements.
Claverings, XXXIV

To all mothers their sons are ever young.
Miss Mackenzie, XIX

To him there came no happy turning-point at which life first loomed seriously on him, and then became prosperous.
Autobiography, III

I am not sure that those whose boyhoods are so protracted have the worst of it ... Fruit that grows ripe the quickest is not the sweetest; nor when housed and garnered will it keep the longest.
Orley Farm, III

Young men ... are more inclined to be earnest and thoughtful when alone than they ever are when with others ... I fancy that, as we grow old ourselves, we are apt to forget that it was so with us ... We constantly talk of the thoughtlessness of youth. I do not know whether we might not more appropriately speak of its thoughtfulness.
Small House at Allington, XIV

Young men are pretty much the same everywhere, I guess. They never have their wits about them. They never mean what they say, because they don't understand the use of words. They are generally half impudent and half timid ... Indeed there is no such thing as a young man, for a man is not really a man till he is middle-aged.
Duke's Children, XXXIII

Solitude is surely for the young, who have time before them ... and who can, therefore, take delight in thinking.
Last Chronicle of Barset, XLIX

Men & Gentlemen

The one great line of demarcation in the world was that which separated gentlemen from non-gentlemen ... He [a clergyman] would probably have have said that the line of demarcation came just below himself.

'Two Heroines of Plumplington'

A perfect gentleman is a thing which I cannot define.

Last Chronicle of Barset, XLII

He was a born gentleman, which is so great a recommendation for a Radical. *Ralph the Heir*, XX

The one offence which a gentleman is supposed never to commit is that of speaking an untruth. The offence may be one committed oftener than any other by gentlemen, as also by all other people. *Eustace Diamonds*, XXIX

A profession ... signified a calling by which a gentleman, not born to the inheritance of a gentleman's allowance of good things, might ingeniously obtain the same by some exercise of his abilities. *Bertrams*, VIII

A man will dine, even though his heart be breaking.

Small House at Allington, XXVIII

There is great doubt as to what may be the most enviable time of life with a man. I am inclined to think that it is at that period when his children have all been born but have not yet begun to go astray or to vex him with disappointment; when his own pecuniary prospects are settled ... when the appetite is still good and the digestive organs at their full power; when he has ceased to care as to the length of his girdle, and before the doctor warns him against solid breakfasts and port wine after dinner; when his affections are over and his infirmities have not yet come upon him ... As regards men, this, I think, is the happiest time of life; but who shall answer the question as regards women? *Orley Farm*, LIX

There is a baldness that is handsome and noble, and a baldness that is peculiarly mean and despicable.

Ralph the Heir, XXII

Mr Palliser had been brought up in a school which delights in tranquillity, and never allows its pupils to commit themselves either to the sublime or to the ridiculous.

Small House at Allington, LV

The sick birds, we are told, creep into holes, that they may die alone ... A man has the same instinct to conceal the weakness of his sufferings; but, if he be a man, he hides it in his own heart ... while to the outer world he carries a face on which his care has made no mark.

Belton Estate, XVI

Let a man undertake what duty he will in life, if he be a good man he will desire success; and if he be a brave man he will long for victory.

Landleaguers, XXXIX

Take them as a whole, the nobility of England are pleasant acquaintances to have ... It's simply growing up, towards the light, as trees do.   *Can You Forgive Her?*, XXI

Manliness is not compatible with affectation ... An affected man ... may be honest, may be generous, may be pious; but surely he cannot be manly. The self-conscious assumption of any outward manner ... is fatal ... Let a man put his hat down, and you shall say whether he has deposited it with affectation or true nature.

Phineas Redux, LXVIII

Little men in authority are always stern.

The Vicar of Bullhampton, LXVI

A man cannot change as men change. Individual men are like the separate links of a rotatory chain. The chain goes on with continuous easy motion as though every part of it were capable of adapting itself to a curve, but ... each link [is] as stiff and sturdy as any other piece of wrought iron.

Rachel Ray, XVIII

Money & Work

It is not the prize that can make us happy; it is not even the winning of the prize ... [it is] the struggle, the long hot hour of the honest fight ... There is no human bliss equal to twelve hours of work with only six hours in which to do it.

Orley Farm, XLIX

The more a man earns the more useful he is to his fellow-men.

Autobiography, VI

A man who cannot take off his hat to his work, and pay it reverence, is not a workman in a happy frame of mind.

Lecture, 'The Civil Service as a Profession', 1861

[After Longman's argued that he should remain with their old firm]: 'It is for you,' said he, 'to think whether our names on your title-page are not worth more to you than the increased payment.' This seemed to me to savour of that high-flown doctrine of the contempt of money which I have never admired. I did think much of Messrs. Longman's name, but I liked it best at the bottom of a cheque.

Autobiography, VI

Oh the City, the weary City, where men go daily to look for money, but find none.

Three Clerks, XXXVI

In some insidious unforeseen manner, in a way that can only be understood after much experience, these luxuries of fashion do make a heavy pull on a modest income.

Eustace Diamonds, XXXII

When we talk of sordid gain and filthy lucre, we are generally hypocrites.

Thackeray, 44

There are faces which, in their usual form, seem to bluster with prosperity.

Eustace Diamonds, XXVIII

You know what I mean by good living. It is not simply beef and pudding, though they form no inconsiderable part of it. It is education, religion without priestcraft, political freedom, the power and habit of thinking, the capacity for enjoying life like a man, instead of enduring life like a brute. Lecture, 'The Present Condition of the
Northern States of the American Union', 1862

There is hardly a pleasure in life equal to that of laying out money with a conviction that it will come back again. The conviction, alas, is so often ill founded, but the pleasure is the same. *Ralph the Heir*, XLIX

The man who is insensible to the power money brings with it must be a dolt.

Lady Anna, IV

'If honest men did not squabble for money, in this wicked world of ours, the dishonest men would get it all; and I do not see that the cause of virtue would be much improved.' *Barchester Towers*, XIV

Competition, that beautiful science of the present day, by which every plodding cart-horse is converted into a racer. *Struggles of Brown, Jones, and Robinson*, V

[On a parvenu's country house]: 'Very grand; but the young trees show the new man. A new man may buy a forest; but he can't get park trees.'

Phineas Finn, XIV

He knew that work alone could preserve him from sinking – hard, constant, unflinching work, that one great cure for all our sorrow, that only means of adapting ourselves to God's providences. *Bertrams*, XXXIII

A man cannot leave his work for ever without some touch of melancholy. *Mr Scarborough's Family*, LVIII

[A lady to a painter]: 'I am told that all you do is successful now, merely because you do it. That is the worst of success … That when won by merit it leads to further success for the gaining of which no merit is necessary.'

Last Chronicle of Barset, LI

The natural, I may say, the only happy condition of a man is to work for his living.

Unpublished lecture, 'Zulus & Zululand', 1879

It is the nature of man to appreciate his own work.

John Caldigate, XLVII

There are men who love work, who revel in that, who attack it daily with renewed energy, almost wallowing in it, greedy of work, who go to it almost as the drunkard goes to his bottle, or the gambler to his gaming-table. These are not unhappy men, though they are perhaps apt to make those around them unhappy.   *Ralph the Heir*, LI

Who can doubt but that work is the great civilizer of the world – work and the growing desire for those good things which work only will bring?

South Africa, 'Kimberley'

Parents & Children

The hold of a child upon the father is so much stronger than that of the father on the child! Our eyes are set in our face, and are always turned forward. The glances that we cast back are but occasional.

Sir Harry Hotspur, XVI

Fathers … hardly ever give sufficient credit to the remorse which young men feel when they gradually go astray.

Ralph the Heir, VIII

[A father giving way to his son]: As the sun is falling in the heavens and the evening lights come on, this world's wealth and prosperity afford no pleasure equal to this. It is this delight that enables a man to feel, up to the last moment, that the goods of the world are good.

Ralph the Heir, XI

In no condition of life can justice be more imperatively due than from a father to his son.

Duke's Children, VII

A grown-up son must be the greatest comfort a man can have, if he be his father's best friend; but otherwise he can hardly be a comfort. *Phineas Finn*, XI

How many a miserable father reviles with bitterness of spirit the low tastes of his son, who has done nothing to provide his child with higher pleasures!

Doctor Thorne, XXVIII

I am glad you are to have a child. One wants some one to exercise unlimited authority over, as one gets old and cross. Letter, 5 Oct. 1852

Food

Our finer emotions should always be encouraged with a stomach moderately full. *Bertrams*, VI

'Adam and Eve were in paradise. Why? Their digestion was good. Ah! then they took liberties, ate bad fruit, things they could not digest … Ah, to digest is to be happy.'

Claverings, XIX

I confess … that I like wine … it seems to me that my dinner goes down better with a glass of sherry than without it. *North America*, I.iii

We are often told in our newspapers that England is disgraced by this and by that; by the unreadiness of our army, by the unfitness of our navy, by the irrationality of our laws, by the immobility of our prejudices, and what not; but the real disgrace of England is the railway sandwich, that whited sepulchre, fair enough outside, but so meagre, poor, and spiritless within ...

He Knew He Was Right, XXXVII

I love to have my tea-cup emptied and filled with gradual pauses, so that time for oblivion may accrue, and no exact record be taken. *North America*, I.iii

A man always dines, let his sorrow be what it may. A woman contents herself with tea, and mitigates her sorrow, we must suppose, by an extra cup.

Old Man's Love, IX

Ladies, though they like good things at picnics, and indeed, at other times ... very seldom prepare dainties for themselves alone. Men are wiser and more thoughtful, and are careful to have the good things, even if they are to be enjoyed without companionship.

He Knew He Was Right, XVI

A picnic should be held among green things. Green turf is absolutely an essential ... There should certainly be hills and dales ... and, above all, there should be running water.

Can You Forgive Her? VIII

[Christmas requires] a fine old English dinner at three o'clock – a sirloin of beef a foot and a half broad, a turkey as big as an ostrich, a plum pudding bigger than the turkey, and two or three dozen mince pies.

'Christmas at Thompson Hall'

'You seem to have a good appetite, Mr Trollope' [said a lady at a dinner party]. 'Not at all, madam, but, thank God, I am very greedy.'

Michael Sadleir, *Trollope: A Commentary*, 331

Old Age

It is sad for a man to feel, when he knows that he is fast going down the hill of life … [that] by some unconscious and unlucky leap he has passed from the unripeness of youth to the decay of age, without even knowing what it was to be in his prime.

Castle Richmond, XXXV

My young friend! thou art ignorant in this – as in most other things … that old man's heart is as soft as thine, if thou couldst but read it. The body dries up and withers away, and the bones grow old; the brain, too, becomes decrepit … But the heart that is tender once remains tender to the last.

Orley Farm, XXVI

Years do not make a man old gradually and at an even pace. Look through the world and see if this is not so always, except in those rare cases in which the human being lives and dies without joys and without sorrows, like a vegetable. A man shall be possessed of florid youthful blooming health till, it matters not what age. Thirty – forty – fifty, then comes some nipping frost, some period of agony, that robs the fibres of the body of their succulence, and the hale and hearty man is counted among the old.

Barchester Towers, XXXII

Now in his green old age … [Archdeacon Grantly] had ceased to covet, but had not ceased to repine.

Last Chronicle of Barset, II

Excitement is a great step towards happiness particularly to those who are over sixty.

Blackwoods, May 1877

As a man grows old he wants amusement, more even than when he is young; and then it becomes so difficult to find amusement.

Autobiography, IX

[Success]: As we grow old things seem to come so quickly!
John Caldigate, XLI

The Earl had been a man quite capable of making himself disagreeable ... Of all of our capabilities this is the one which clings longest to us.   *Phineas Redux*, XI

A man does, in truth, remember that which it interests him to remember; and when we hear that memory has gone as age has come on, we should understand that the capacity for interest in the matter has perished. A man will be generally very old and feeble before he forgets how much money he has in the funds.   *Autobiography*, IX

I fear I have lost the hearing of one ear ... Why should anything go wrong in our bodies? Why should we not be all beautiful? Why should there be decay? – why death? – and, oh, why damnation? the last we get out of by not believing it.   Letter, 9 Oct. 1873

A man's ideas of generosity change as he advances in age.
Claverings, XLIV

[Mr Harding's face]: There was very much melancholy in it, of that soft sadness of age which seems to acknowledge, and in some sort to regret, the waning oil of life; but the regret to be read in such faces has in it nothing of the bitterness of grief; there is no repining that the end has come, but simply a touch of sorrow that so much that is dear must be left behind.   *Last Chronicle of Barset*, XLII

The juices of life had been pressed out of him; his thoughts were all of his cares and never of his hopes.
Miss Mackenzie, IX

The Author's Farewell

We are going ever with our lives in our hands, knowing that death is common to all of us; and knowing also, for all of us who ever think do know it, that to him who dies death must be horrible or blessed, not in accordance with an hour or two of final preparation, but as may be the state of the dying man's parting soul as the final result of the life which he has led.   *Travelling Sketches*, 108

I have no fear of death itself, but only the long wait for it. When once a man has made up his mind that God means to do him good, he ceases to fear death.

Guardian, 11 Dec. 1882

Now I stretch out my hand, and from the further shore I bid adieu to all who have cared to read any among the many words that I have written.

Autobiography, XX